PEN…POETRY… PURPOSE

SHATAWN REID

Purposefully Write Publishing, LLC

PEN…POETRY… PURPOSE

CONTENT

4 LETTER WORD

The greatest word to ever be constructed,
consisting of 4 letters that can be used as an emotion
but doubles as an action.
Simultaneously raising a wanting of an embrace
while giving someone the strength to lay down their
life for another.
It narrows sight so that only the spec of perfection
can be seen in the midst of flaws.
Unconditionally forgetting all the wrongs
that have been done
so that one can carry on.
When this word is put into motion,
it can pluck out the signs of hatred and allow peace
to be the foundation.

It can allow an operation to be done in your soul
to mend the holes that were developed
by past trauma, failures, and mistakes.
It's industrially strong with the ability to
plaster forgiveness on the heart of the misused and abused.
In the heat of heartbreak and pain,
it's the midst of a gentle summer rain
extinguishing the fire that tries to burn you.

The first sight of a new dawn knowing that new mercies
have been renewed for you live another day.
It crushes transgressions to dust to be use to bloom
a fresh new anointing.

This 4-letter word is word LOVE.
And it's by a 3-letter word that love can be described...
it is GOD.
And His example of when emotion meets action is when
He gave His one and only Son,
Jesus for the masses so that we could have the opportunity
to always be in His presence.
While we yet are not knowledgeable of better,
He made a plan so that we could be better through the
death and acknowledgement of a Savior.
A noble gesture to save an undeserving people,
now that's love.

Agape.
Unconditional.
It will always be the greatest 4-letter ever constructed
because it is created by the greatest Creator and the reason
for our existence.

A BLACK MAN/I LOVE HIM

He is tall, He is short, He is average height.
He is strong, naturally powerful, unable to make him fall;
He is relentless.
Not a beast, he is gentle.
Mentally able to stand against any man,
he is feared by those who approach him
because they are unaware of his brilliance.
He is smooth;
no swagger like his, no one can match his style.
And I am proud to say that I know him, for he is a black man
and I love him.
For he has come a long way through adversity's journey
to make his presence evident today.
And there are many that hope that he would just go away
but he stays.
Not letting those who hate him make him go astray.
And I'm honored to say I have met him for he is a black man
and I love him.

He has a dark chocolate, milk chocolate, caramel complexion.
Dark or light, it's no guessing of who he is because
it's illuminated when he speaks.
He speaks with authority, confidence, and security of
who he is and what he represents.

And yes,
sometime given a bad rep but only because
they wish they could do it like that.
His hands are marked from molding this land,
planted the seeds for this land to grow.
So the roughness represents the hard and tireless work
to build this nation from the ground up.
But beyond the roughness,
it the smoothness of his hands;
when they place caresses upon the texture of a woman's skin.
It's his touch,
like nothing that can ever be imagined,
smooth yet intense when place upon a woman
that he respects.
And I am passionate when I say;
I can't get enough of a black man's touch because
I love it.
And I love him.
He is a father, a son, a brother, a cousin, an uncle.
He is the brother behind bars that got caught up,
don't worry son because I still love ya.
He is a lawyer, he is a cop working undercover,
he is a husband;
he is a friend.
A man who will be there until the end.
He is handsome, he is gorgeous,
His looks stand out amongst the others,
he is genuine.

Cannot be redesigned or altered;
a true image of God's creation,
from the thickness of the hair down to the
roughness of his feet,
he is complete.
Sculpted for all eyes to see, marvel at his greatness.
He is historical, he is cultural, he is spiritual,
he is a writer of God's destiny and
a poet of life's stories.
For he is a black man and
I love me some him.

So I pay homage to you,
my black men,
for you are wonderful.
I want to make it very clear,
when we as woman utter words of anger;
don't believe what you hear.
For when we are angry,
we can say a lot that can possibly
harden your heart.
But I can place a seal of guarantee,
that no matter what we say, you are our men, our
BLACK MEN AND WE LOVE YOU.

A LETTER TO A GENERATION

As I reflected on the condition of the world,
seeing the shifting that looks to be going on,
I decided to write this letter.
I'm writing this letter to the dearest of those
who are meant to be the regeneration
of a world that seems to be in chaos.
This is for you;
not relying on your skin tone but on
what your future has in store.
You.
Wrapped in a mini posterior but
graced with such vigor.
I see you.
And I admire you as you grow into
what God has injected within you,
like the angel in Heaven who sits
in admiration of the manifestation
of His creation;
it is you that the tone has been set for.

You are here for a reason much bigger
than carnal eyes can see.
Dilate your eyes in order to expand the spectrum
so that can see what the Father's see.

You are designed to bring the charge
into full rotation.
In synagogues,
spreading light in dark places.
Your size is irrelevant to what your
Father has supplied you with.
The example of how we should approach the Kingdom,
already a picture-perfect illustration.
So I wrote this letter to let you know
that you are special.
Your likeness is not like any other
creation among you.
You are a good work in the eyes
of the One who created you.
Your past doesn't define you because
you have a purpose to guide you
and destiny that surrounds you.
Fearfully and wonderfully made;
the world cannot hide you.
The beauty of you penetrates perception if you allow it to
and diminishes the falsehood that
greatness is beyond you.

It is seen and feared,
thus the attempts to make you
believe less than the truth.
The end is the beginning for you.

You are the Joshua's and Caleb's
of this dispensation of the mission.
Set your standards of what you want to see.
Don't compromise because of negativity.
Walk with the boldness given by the Spirit.
Stand firm on what you've been taught.
You are princes and princesses of a King
that sit above all.

And I want you to know that I'm right beside you
with all who believe in you;
supporting you in your journey.
Stay strong in the Lord and the power of
His might that lives within you.

BEAUTIFUL FLOWER

She was planted in the soil of this earth
to be watered and nurtured by the ways of this land.
Surrounded by dirt of hopelessness and worry,
she refused to let it keep her down
and so she grew.
Breaking through the top layer of the world's
discouragement,
she flourished.
And she stood,
weathering the storms of life.
The rain of doubt, the thunderstorms of problems,
the hurricanes of fear
and the tornados of chaos,
she fought through them all and continued to grow.
Continued to show her strength by feeding off
what would otherwise kill and destroy her belief
that she can make it.
That she can take whatever obstacles that may come her way
that would prevent her from persevering
and so she grew.

Extending her limbs to touch the air
while letting the world know that she is here,
she grew.
Standing tall over all that attempted to make her fall,
she grew.

Making her presence known,
showing that she is one of God's greatest creations
and so she grew.
And she bloomed to be a woman of grace and integrity.
This woman that I'm speaking of is me.
This woman that I'm speaking of is you.
She is the single mother on her knees constantly praying
to be what her kids need her to be.
She is a young woman trying to make it in a world
that is said to be created for men
but she shows that she can be as successful
as any man can.
She is the student trying to complete her way through school
when others tell her that she will fail.

She is a beautiful flower,
raised in a meadow filled with beautiful flowers
that have set the pace before her.
Living amongst an array of beautiful flowers
that are traveling this journey with her.
In full bloom,
she has overcome odds
and been set apart for future seeds to admire
the path that she has taken.
Her petals are opened for all eyes to glance
and marvel at her beauty that shows from
the inside out.

To all my beautiful flowers out there,
I say keep growing
and I say keep showing your splendor for others to see.
You have been placed in a position to be example
of what a strong woman should be.
Blossom to full form for this is what God
would have it to be.
Allow the sun to shine upon you so that your beauty
can illuminate amongst the eyes of all who see you.
You are beautiful.
You are precious;
and like a sweet-smelling flower,
continue to send your scent of strength
throughout the earth.
I encourage you to always bloom my sisters,
bloom.

Pressed within like an olive being strained of its nectar,
I pray;
not to drink from this cup
but I knew;
that this was my calling from the foundation of
days existence so that they can have the
opportunity to experience the Father's anointing.
I do this for them.
They...
who I feed with two fish and five loaves of beard
but when asked to choose between myself
and the world they yelled "crucify Him!"
That was the plan and I stand upon the promise
that the Father gave to man,
that a Savior would come to take away their sins,
and although they deny that I am Him,
I do this for them.
I love them.

Mocked for my selflessness to fulfill the Father's will.
Made a spectacle of while they slam a
crown of thorns upon my head.
I take this punishment so that they won't have to
feel the wrath of God's judgment.

Whipped with cattails...
every strike tearing of my flesh so that
they will have a way to fight against theirs.
Blood flowing from the broken veins of my innards...
this blood I shed will carry the solution to life's woe.
I do this for them for I love them so.
My friends...
I call them as I sacrifice myself although
they ignore my presence and refuse to accept me for
who I am.
I carry this cross...
this curse...
that they may live in my Father's grace.
I surrender my life to this conviction.

Path of sorrow I tread as they laugh and scorn me.
"I love you all!"
My heart screams as I look in the eyes our image...
oh God!
The sorrow of this path is not just for me
but for those who decides not to believe.
Nails in my feet... one for each hand.
Pinned down to be hung up for the transgressions of man.
First hour...second hour... third.
Mother, see your son and be proud of Him.
The purpose of my birth is coming to fruition.

The hour is at hand.
Lots casted to see how long I will last.
As long as it takes to defeat the weakness of man.

Fourth hour... fifth hour... sixth.
Darkness covers the sky
but the Son of God will bring marvelous light.
Six...
by one man's disobedience all of creation fell
but by one man's servitude all shall rise out of
the ashes of death into the light of life who believes in Him.
On my left,
hangs the world's systemic way of deception.
On my right,
hangs the truth that as of this day they have
the ability to be with me in paradise.
"Father! Father! Why have you forsaken me?!
You've turned your head so not to see Your begotten die
so dreadfully.
I can't feel Your presence,
disconnected from you so that You can reconnect with them.
Torn veil.
I understand."

I am the lifeline source to rejuvenate their dead existence.
Place of skulls...
can these dry bones live again?!

Through Me they can.
Have mercy on them,
they don't fully understand the divine design.
That they are a part of something that is destined
to give them hope and an expected end.
Seventh hour...eighth hour...ninth.
I could summon a legion of angels to rescue me
but this is not about my desire.
I have to go through this to be appeasing to my Father.
Sacrificial Lamb.
A perfect man I walked this land,
a sinful man I will leave to yet be resurrected with
all power and the keys of death in my possession,
to sit upon my Father's eternal right hand for them.
Intercessor.
I now give of my Spirit, Father.
Your divine Will for me has been completed.
It is finished.
This was my passion to be a road to salvation
for Your creation,
taking the chastisement for their indiscretions.
And even though it was predestined,
I went through this,
I did this because
I love them.

BLACK BEAUTY

There has been a televised revelation about you
that has been cluttered with untruth.
Because your skin radiates with melanin
kissed by the rays of royalty,
the world labels you as a problem.
The fact that you have been given the blessing
to have a chocolate cover skin tone that reads
50 shades of Blackness it is said or presumed that
greatness isn't attached to you.
These lies have been built of the foundation formed for you
to self-destruct while placing the spirit of doubt within
the battlefield of your mind because,
even in the midst of transition from this realm to the next,
they can't help but to speak negatively of who you are.

You were created in the image of a God
who I know for sure makes no mistakes because
His image is pure perfection.
The creation that is you,
He sees as good for with His hands He
fearfully and wonderfully molded you to release
pheromones of purpose and distinction from out
of your pores.
Giving you this mahogany flesh that drips with beauty
because He knew that you can handle it.

For it was by His grace that you have the strength
to endure the ridicule that He already foreseen
would come your way.
Again,
my Father makes no mistakes.
The words of those who don't know you
can only keep you captive
if you allow them to.

The fact that you are cannot be disputed,
even though they try to discredit your existence.
You are a beam remove from the Most High,
placed upon this earth to shine in the midst of darkness
and your complexion,
is a fluorescent wonder,
a sight to behold.
So King,
I want you to know that you are Black Beauty.
Queen,
I want you to know that you are Black Beauty.
And it's not just because of the color of your skin,
but it because of the majestic glow that illuminates from
the inside out,
which shows off the power that God has given you.
Now...let that revelation be televised.

The blessings of the Lord, looks to be continually
overtaking you,
bringing upon you no sorrow.
But it sends a reminder that the Father's mind is ever on you.
He loves you, in an unconditional matter of factual truth.
Your Creator,
who knows you more intricately than you can comprehend,
wants the best for you.
That you would walk in the inherited calling on your life
to have abundant living now and eternal living in the next.

He continues to have something supernaturally up
His sleeve for your good.
And just when you think it can't get any better,
here God goes again showing you that He favors you...
Adores your very existence because you are His chosen;
His property.
In good pleasure,
He steadily upgrades you to make you more valuable
than He already sees you.
Your price tag contains an amount that cannot be numbered,
paid by the life of a Savior who is His only begotten Son,
Jesus.

And if that doesn't confirm in your spirit that you are
precious in His sight,
nothing ever will.
There is nothing in this world that can out measure
the love of the One who's able.
He is a Continual God who continuously
shows forth His grace in the lives of His beloved and,
as long as we have breath to breathe,
He will continually be the Great God that He is.

I AM BLACK HISTORY

What was meant to curse a people,
to oppress a people that ten to look a little different in
fleshly attire,
strengthen a people.
Designed to be a dream deferred but became a dream that
emerged from the tyranny of captivity.
I know why the caged bird sings,
singing a song of victory in the confines of what seemed
to be tragedy.
My people,
three-part beings with the outer layer being
a bit darker than what perception sometimes sees fit
to be acceptable,
took what was thought to be a forced concept
and received revelation of their greatness.
Through their faith in the Creator,
they understood the concept that they are
fearfully and wonderfully made in an image of glory
no matter what the shade.

Never ceasing,
and because of their pressing,
we are now able to see that God was making a way for us
to become that in which He made.

He had a plan from the beginning
for He's intentional that way.
By way of witty inventions and determination to see change,
by His grace,
the Lord allowed a people to open up pathways.
The harder the enemy attempted to diminish their faith
and block their stride;
He only gave reason for them to believe much stronger...
To pray much deeper and to stand much taller as they held
onto God's unchanging hand.
For upon the mountaintop,
they saw the promise for a better tomorrow
for those who would follow.

They continued to fight the good fight of their faith
by holding on to the only message that matter,
"God will always make a way."
And in the midst of the valley of discrimination,
there was a midst of beauty in the form of a lily
and His name is Jesus;
for not by any means because He is the only means
that is necessary.
We celebrate those who stood the gap for truth:
Martin Luther King, Jr., Medgar Evans, Harriet Tubman,
Sojourner Truth;
and we celebrate those who embraced the gifts and talents
given to them by the Father to be creators, scholars,
and artists:

Maya Angelou, Langston Hughes, Garrett A. Morgan,
Madam C.J. Walker, W.E.B. DuBois, and many more.

We celebrate them,
not just because of the color of their skin,
but because of the content of their character as they
pressed their way out of the mouth of persecution into
the hands of God's grace while embracing God's mercy.
They laid the foundation as they became Black History,
so that we could become Black History,
for the Black History that is yet still to come.

JUST A TOUCH

"Who touched me?"
It is I Master, I...
who is not even worthy to eat upon the crumbs underneath
your table.
With my hand stretched,
I fought through the crowd of adversity,
through the calamity surrounding me for the opportunity
to partake of Your virtue.
Life for me has not been a field of daisies;
I've been suffering...
in desert of despair with these infirmities flowing out of me.
Years of toiling in my insufficiencies,
encountering the worse that living seemed to offer.
Spent of myself, in effort to place together the puzzle
of what looked to be my reality only to realize that
there was a piece missing for completion.

Attempted to be a mender of the broken glass of my past
but my Elmer's glue wouldn't hold its seal
and my masking tape tore apart separating me
further from what I needed...
healing.
Detached from wholeness...
scattered,
unable to find the return to sender to my peace.

Searched all over to friends and family to help rescue me
but I was only shunned because to them I was spoiled by
my circumstances,
leaving a stench that they didn't want to be around.
In a hopeless place,
I laid in a puddle of my mess until I heard that there was One,
who carries renewal in His hands.
His voice conveys commands so when He speaks,
disorder comes to a standstill.
Out of His pores extracts the very essence of perfection.
Purity is His designer label
and forgiveness is His forever fragrance.

And I believed from within that if I could just get a touch
of Your power to connect with my faith,
I would be made whole again.
That You would remove the stains of destruction
from my being so that I can live in the
totality of the time.
I had nothing to lose
but freedom from my condition to gain.
My soul was on E and You made me full on the diesel of hope.
The shade of anguish had made me blind but
You uncovered to me truth,
giving me the sight to see a brighter journey ahead.
You are the light,

and I just needed to get in contact with the rays of Your shine
in order to build the strength of my bones
to stand on the truth that I have purpose.

So yes Lord,
it was I who touch Your glory.
I just needed to forgo my fear to be consumed in
Your presence.
Please forgive me.
"No my Child,
your faith has made you whole.
Go in peace.
Your suffering is over."

LIFE MATTERS

Hashtags have become a symbol of acknowledgement
of a person not known before their soul detached
from their body by way of a piece of fiery steel piercing
their skin.
Leaving wounds upon a community doomed to repeat
the scene all over again.
From their bloodshed,
dried on the pavement of the perception on whether or not
the world would be better off without them.
You can hear the cries of their spirit asking,
"Did my life really ever matter?"
Not discriminatory of gender but the melanin
that covers that which gave shelter to who
they really were.

That which gave their existence meaning and cause;
because they were created before they were formed
with a Heavenly intent.
Dreams and vision that were etched upon their hearts
now buried and emerged in the depths
of muddy grounds,
corpses with no chance to grow into
a chance for change.
And why?
Why should my outer manifestation be the catalyst
for my life's premature expiration?

Black Lives Matter.
But the explanation of my creation should not be
predicated on the nature of my skin tone.
Not by the dialect of my speech or the tradition from
which I've grown.

I am an artistic abstract made with the hands
of a connoisseur of creating things of specialty.
We as a race of humanity were designed to give life
to what would otherwise be vegetation.
Our Creator sculpted us to be the best part of Him,
that's why He made us in the image of Him.
Giving us gifts and talents beneficial to His purpose,
to live our lives in His grace with the abundance
of His promises.
We are fearfully and wonderfully made differently
to be the same.
Our beginning and our end should not be based upon
our outer texture but by our willingness to be
what we were created to be.
Greatness is the true fate of us.

We are brothers and sisters cut from different cloths
to make an existence of beauty.
And only when we redirect our mental to this
ingenious awareness,
can the perceive notion of anything other than that die never
to be resurrected again.

My past ran up on me the other day.
And placed in my memory the person I use to be.
Reminding me of the times that I strayed away and
made decisions on my own.
How my life started to crumble as if it was being destroyed
by a cyclone.
It reminded me when depression sat in and I thought about
bringing my life to an end.
It was playing in my thoughts like a movie on a movie screen,
while in my ear,
it began to whisper to me,
"I, your past, have made your future.
Because of me,
your dreams will never be.
So I applaud you on the decisions that you're made,
for it because of your choices,
your life has been placed in the grave."

I declared to him,
I don't know what you think you know,
but past,
I'm sorry but you have to go.
You have no place to take up space in my mental.
Trying to hold land in the field of my mind to make me
think that I'm finished.

I am a vessel
and those thoughts are unwanted cargo that I'm tossing
overboard into the sea of forgetfulness.
You are my end,
because I have a new beginning and I want to inform you that
you're not in it.
I was a sinner,
but by God's grace,
I am now a saint.
And those things you're trying to bring up have been
thrown away.
New slate.
Because my Father has forgiven me
and paved the way for me to be what
He has prearranged for me to be.
His mercies are everlasting and He has had mercy on me.
I am His child, and I have an inheritance for me to succeed.
I won't allow you to dictate my future,
to kill my dreams by slashing it at the seams.
Cause I'm suited up by grace and protected by favor.
There is no room for you to make me waver.

I won't give you the satisfaction of looking back.
I'm too tall and you're too small to even give you eye contact.
I will walk all over you with my feet because you are
beneath me.
I am a part of the Royal Family of GOD, so you should
fear me.

Never again will you have rule over me.
Now flee from me you enemy, go about your way.
In Christ Jesus, I always have a brighter day.
All old things have passed away;
New creature.
Through Christ I have overcome and all my battles have
already been won.
Your days of controlling me are officially done
because I have a race to run and
I won't stop until His will is done.
I am moving forward.

NOT GUILTY

Standing before the Judge,
shackled at the feet and hands making it impossible
to run the race given and to show the appearance
that everything that I touch will fail,
I was sentenced.
In front of a jury filled with naysayers, haters, and people
who were against my maturity, the prosecutor accused me
of the sins that I did commit.
Stating that I was not fit to exist upon this earthly realm
and I was punishable by the Law.
That I should be sentenced to an eternity of death by way
of fiery demise without death ever coming.
The gavel hit and I thought that was it,
but someone came to my defense.

He offered His services to place an appeal on my behalf
and when I asked what was the cost,
He told me that the price was paid upon a wooden cross.
He said that "your final judgment I can change for I have
a relationship with the Judge.
I am His Son, Jesus.
And if you place your trust in Me and your life in My hands,
I guarantee your sentence will be reversed."

So I gave Him everything of me;
my sins, my soul, my hurt, my heart and trusted that He will
be a Man of His word seeing that He is the Word
born into flesh.
Back before the Judge I returned with the One who died
and rose again...
my Defense.
He approached the bench and began to say, "Your Honor,
My Master,
Abba Father,
I come to You interceding on behalf of this Your daughter;
that her sentence will be overturned;
that she can be all that You called for her to be.

Look at these wounds upon my body,
I took them for her transgressions.
These bruises upon my flesh for her iniquities.
I was chastened that she may have peace and by these stripes,
she can be spiritually healed.
So Your Honor,
I come to You to reverse her sentence from death to life,
for all who are in Me can have life and have it abundantly."
The prosecutor continued to accuse me of my past.
When the Judge spoke He said,
"I, God, rebuke you, accuser. For this is My Son,
in whom I am well pleased and because of Him,
I have forgiven her of her sins."

Once dressed in filthy rags as a prisoner of my wrongs,
now clothed in garments of cleanness and righteousness.
No longer will be bound by my infirmities.
Because of Christ, I can walk this life with a verdict of
NOT GUILTY!

PEN...POETRY...PURPOSE

When given a task to paint upon a canvas,
pure white,
with words that will impact a people,
you must understand the assignment.
Not gifted for amusement,
but to dilute the falsehood that has plagued the world since
the beginning of time.
Transferring words into a message meant to penetrate
the ears of the hearing and the eyes of the seeing.
Are you willing to embrace it?
Giving encouragement and hope to what seems
to be a dying generation.

Fiction situations dictated in a way that can be
translated to be understood by all nations.
Speaking of God's grace to save the world from
itself by the sacrifice of His Son,
Jesus.
The nourishment needed for spirits and souls of those
that roam this Earth,
moaning and groaning for more;
more than what sight sees.
Inserts faith that provides hope to the hopeless,
meat that sticks to the ribs of the heart forever.

Being injected by the well that never runs dry,
the gift placed in the hands of those who are willing to
accept the calling,
helps to quench the thirst of man.

Given a pen to be use like a filter to allow the poetry
to flow as strong as water through a storm pipe,
cleansing all that is within its touch.
This purpose goes far beyond self because
it affords the opportunity for the Father
to be heard while using the gift as a vessel.
Inspiration is the motivation.
Spreading a message of Good News
is the mission.
For when given a PEN with the ability to create POETRY,
the only PURPOSE you have is to put the world on notice
that they can be free.

R.I.P (REST IN PEACE)

R.I.P.
An acronym used in association to someone who has
transitioned from this life to the next.
Simplistic in its meaning,
we incline to say that the person is now at rest because
no more do they have to endure the troubles that life
seems to bring.
That they have entered into a peaceful state of ease
amongst their soul,
not having to worry about the things of this world anymore.
Rest in Peace.
But what if I told you that this feeling could be obtained
while yet in the land of the living?
That you can,
not only have rest from within,
but also have the peace that surpasses mere
carnal understanding.

This dynamic duo destroys the depiction of confusion
and devastation through their direct relations with the One
who is able to save.
Cut from the same cloth,
you can't experience one without experiencing the other.
They are promises given upon salvation when the Savior

revived your spirit and renewed you soul to be
blameless before God's throne.
When you are in His rest,
you have the ability to remove the boulders of heavy-laden
that have collapsed upon you like an avalanche from
the steepest mountain.
Giving your troubles over to the Master while yet
pressing towards the mark of the high calling,
you will be burden free and your steps will be lightened.

His peace is like being in a raging storm but you are laying
soundly upon a pillow in the vessel of life;
no stressing, knowing that your Captain is in control.
Know that this is obtainable right where you are.
I'm talking to my blood-soaked believers.
Those who have been covered by God's grace and cocooned
in His mercy to grow wings as eagles,
to blossom to live this life abundantly
and one day live in the everlasting.
Because,
to be honest,
if your life isn't connected to the life source that is the Christ
then your soul will never truly be able to enter
into this place.
But that's another subject for a different piece.

These well-stitched promises allow you to walk this life
without the soles of your feet being worn
and the clothes of your soul being torn.

To know that if it feels like your feet can't touch
dry land that,
like a dove,
these promises will provide a branch of reassurance that
God is with you and your victory is inevitable.
They allow patience to have its perfect work in you
in the midst of trying times.
And the promise to enter into this state still stands
however, it is your choice to want to reach it.
So my brothers and sisters,
those who with a willingness to receive,
with all my heart and love towards you,
I bid you to Rest in Peace.

SOMETIMES

A smile on the face can at times be a mask of
what's really going on from within.
Covering up the realness of the person
so that they can walk with the perception
of being strong.
I know this feeling all too well.
I am a living testament of it.
With a smile,
you will never know the times when I had those
moments of "sometimes"
Because sometimes,
I felt like I was being murdered from within
by a machine gun shooting my spirit with
no chance of being revived.
Sometimes,
I felt like I was being ripped apart from my soul
by way of a sword,
slicing me to the core while I attempt to hold on.
Sometimes,
I felt like this Christian life I live was in vain
because of all the heartache and pain that continuously
reigns as days go by.
Sometimes,
I felt like I was living a lie because,
in the course of the pain,

all I could manage to do is cry so hard that
blood would flow from my eyes.
Sometimes,
I felt like I was living more of my emotions instead of
what I was supposed to.
And those sometimes,
sometimes happened
too often than always.

Sometimes,
I could truly understand the Savior's pain
while in the garden of Gethsemane when He yelled...
"FATHER PLEASE TAKE THIS CUP FROM ME!"
And upon the cross as He cried...
"FATHER WHY HAS THOU FORSAKEN ME!"
Because sometimes,
it felt like God had turned His back on me...
while He slowly took His hands off me.
Sometimes,
I felt alone with no one around to comfort me...
couldn't hear the Holy Spirit because my spiritual ears
had been infected from the disease of the fiction
ingested by the enemy that I would never be anything.
Sometimes,
I felt like giving up...
walking away from life itself because
I felt like no one would care.

And those sometimes,
sometimes happened far
too often than always.

But it's at those times,
I continued to press pass the mess in front of me
and force my way through.
At those times,
God showed himself...
showing that He had never left me
because that is what He promised.
At those times,
I made my way around the wall that blocked me seven times
and gave a loud shout of praise until it came
tumbling down.
Understanding that I was sitting outside the gate and,
if I could just make it to the city,
it will be beautiful.
It is at those times,
I mustard up all the strength I had left while the Lord
provided the rest and fought pass those "sometimes"
that caused me stress.
Not comprehending why I had to go through them
but remembering that this life was not meant to be easy.
But sometimes,
I really wish that it could be.

And those sometimes,
sometimes happens
too often than always.
But at those times,
it's confirmed to me that if it were easy,
it wouldn't mean as much when
I walked into victory.

I see you,
as you stand at the edge of the cliff in this situation
wanting to make it to the other side.
With your eyes,
you see the path as an unsteady tight rope that
seems impossible to take.
This path towards your victory that seems to have
too many obstacles to face.
So you cry out to Me and,
make no mistake,
I can hear you for your cries are in tune with my ears.
And your fears,
that lay heavy within your heart,
I hear clearly because I am eternally in tune with its sound.
There's no need to send an APB for me...
I am always present.
Check my attendance on your life's roll book,
I have never been absent.

You must understand that My silence doesn't mean
that I have left you.
The teacher is simply being respectful as the
student takes the test.
My beloved,

I have covered you with my umbrella of grace
that is able to keep you from falling.
And if you manage to stumble,
My word is the safety net underneath your feet
that will prevent you from falling.
I'm the possible in the midst of impossibility
because all things can be done through me.
Just trust Me.
Abide your faith in Me so that we can band together
to make one sound that causes the weather around you
to be still.

My spirit lives inside of you,
so in the midst of your weakest moments,
you are the strongest you've ever been.
I made you to stand the test of eternity.
So be strong and of great courage.
Be on your guard,
remain steadfast and immovable.
Ignore what you see and place your confidence in Me
because that's how the courage within you will arise.
Carnal minded people may not comprehend your stance
because I'm the subliminal message in the center of
distress that carnal minds can't fathom.
But I can assure you that no matter what the circumstance
may be,
I will give you what you need to
stand courageously.

STORY CRY

When she cries and a tear leaves her eye,
it tells a story.
Not of victory or glory but a story of pain and misery.
Loneliness,
self-worthlessness,
and lack of confidence in her ability to be;
the discouragement that she has felt throughout her life.
They say when one cries it is weakness leaving the body.
She continues to cry to gain the strength inside to survive
through this autobiography of her life's mishaps,
mistakes, and journey
Through the lonely feeling
and consist worry in her heart that separates her
from the here and now because back then,
she was told that she wasn't beautiful.

By the first man in her life that she encountered,
her father.
She accepts rejection because she feels that
it's just a reflection of what has already been
told to her.
And yes,
she is now of the age where she can realize
the lies that have been told to her
in the past

And she has gain more of herself as she
attempts to ignore the inner voice
that says that she will never win.
But she worries that her past has already
dictated her future.
She realizes that the biggest fight she has to confront
is within herself.

Because her main enemy and critic
is herself;
and she must prove to herself that
she worth living.
Her heart and her mind have planted
and water the concept that she is nothing.
The task to prove uproot those perceptions will be
a difficult challenge for her.
People you can completely disregard,
but dealing with who you are...
now that's hard.
And she continues cries,
each tear telling a new story.
She is supposed to get stronger,
but all she feels is weakness.
As the tears run down her face,
it's as if she's watering a field of sweet flowers;
but all she sees is dirt around her.
These feelings she must defeat in order
to live her life completely.
She is in a room full of people and all she sees is her.

Greatest story ever told,
is told through her tears,
her cries to be free of this pain.
She is a piece of coal being pressed so
that she can one day appear as a diamond.
The amount of time it will take is unknown,
but how beautiful it will be once she is revealed
as her true form.
So take a lesson from her pain,
of her story of truth.
For this girl that I'm speaking about
probably was or is you.

THAT DAY

It was on that day...
after being stripped of His flesh.
Whipped for the transgressions of those who
He loved but yelled for Him to be put to death.
It was on that day...
after being injection by the disease of sin,
taking that place those who deserved the punishment
much more than Him.
It was on that day...
the day He declared would happen in order
to show the power of the Master.
That He will love us with His life
and with His life He would give
to save ours.

Taking on the task to carry a curse to eliminate
the curse that had been plaguing a people since
the beginning of time.
A way of escape that was made before
time existed
and He was it.
Upon the hill of Calvary,
He fulfilled a promise that the forefathers spoke of
but wouldn't be able to experience.

It was on that day...
after His blood flowed from His body.
Soaking us with the nutrients of its power to restore.
After being pinned up...
becoming the true representation of salvation.
Stretched wide to bridge the gap that had
been destroyed,
stretched long to reconnect us to who we can now
declare as our Father again.

It was on that day...
after His actions affirmed that we are
worth saving.
He became the definition of selflessness
that Webster and Oxford seemed to choose
to omit.
He defined all natural understanding of what
we thought should be and showed us love
unconditional.
It was on that day...
after being wrapped in cloth because of
His submission to the Father's will,
He rose.
Demonstrating that we can die but yet live again
with divine power.

On that day,
He opened up the chance for those who will dare
to believe to be a part of a Heavenly inheritance
and displaying that death no longer
has a sting.
It was on that day,
that the prophecy was realized
and out of the tomb our Savior lives.

THE AWAKENING

There is a sound resonating in the atmosphere.
Can you hear it?
Like police sirens ringing racing to an impending tragedy.
Can you hear it?
The level is deafening;
listen to its message.
Hear the souls of those longing for more than
just their surroundings.
The screams of the hearts seeking fulfillment
but blazing with disappointment,
hatred of the life that they were given by Him;
hear them.
They echo the inquiry,
"Where is this God when we need Him?";
while the appearance of better seems futile.
Can you hear it? Them?
Those...
who have been consumed by the perception perceived
by sight seen in 3D,
damaging,
destructive,
and deceiving.

Yet redemption is found in Jesus according to John 3:16.
By Him we all live,
move,
and have being.
There is no way but through Him
for He is that only way that was made.
And I know that it may sound a bit cliché
but it's the best way for it to be explained.
We as His body are mandated to make His presence known
in fleshly tone in this world
but I must beg the question
"Are we?"
Are we presenting our lives as a product of His grace
or do we live our life presenting His grace as a disgrace?
Are we going forth making disciples, Matt 28:19
or are we sitting back with a heartbeat of
complacency saying,
"If it doesn't directly concern me why face it?"
We seem to operate in the very nature of what
we speak against.
So comfortable in the box we have formed around us,
to step out might seem
quite blasphemous.

The alarm is resounding,
the vibrations are shaking our foundation;
why do we remain blind to it?

We've been napping,
moving as we feel instead of as
Christ ambassador.
We have been given the anointing to pull the lost out
of the hell fire into the consuming fire
to purify their souls.
Fighting for the Kingdom of God knowing that
the fight is rigged.
But if we understand this,
why do we stand in the corner of the ring
taking blows to our spirit?
Concerning ourselves to fit in,
for the road to riches and diamond rings.
While the unsaved are living in the spirit of Eve,
hearing that they won't die as the world
is killing them.

The alarm is ringing and we've pressed snooze
for too long.
It's time to stand on our feet,
on the rock of our salvation,
and speak the truth no matter what the
worldly consequences because to suffer
for truth is to gain.
We've been touched by the hands of the Father
to be boisterous about the Gospel;
to let the world know that being a true Christian
isn't lame.

Not to stand on the sideline and watch but,
in love, proclaim that God loves you
but your sins you must change.
Why chase after death that doesn't
care about you anyway?
We can't be fooled by what we see,
we must operate in the transformation
we experience daily.
And if you are offended maybe you needed to be.
Because it is time get out of the bed
of our complacency.
It is the Awakening.
Please wake up.

UNSTOPPABLE

They say she will never fulfill her dreams.
That she does not have the zeal to succeed,
she will not go far.
Not reach the heavens and touch the stars,
she is hopeless.
Not focus enough to be that diamond in the rough
that comes out to shine
and she doesn't have the strength to climb up
the stairway to sit amongst the best,
she's a mess.
A waste of brain power that can be used in better ways
And it's amazing that she has stayed around
attempting to be what she will never
achieve to be.
She will fall short,
unable to stand tall
and preserver through all that is
to come her way.

Well I say,
I hear you
and all the disbelief that you have made
about my abilities to survive the tasks
that are ahead of me.

I have soaked your words inside of me to arrive
to an appropriate response to you
and your feelings of my ability to be successful.
THANK YOU!
I know that you are hoping that I fail.
That I will fall flat on my face,
upon the pavement of my ambitions
and goals so that you will be right.
WRONG!
For I refuse to wave my white flag and surrender,
I'm not a quitter.
This is a war;
and I plan to win every battle.

Since my desire is to be a warrior,
I will have to let you down.
I will accomplish every goal that I have set
in order to sit amongst the rest.
I will dodge every dagger that you try
to throw at my dreams.
Your words are just evidence of your fear
of my abilities to great.
The fear that I will become that
which you want to hate.
The one that you toot your nose up at
as if you are smelling something foul.
I'm sorry that you didn't know then,
but you know now,
that I will always be around.

I dare you to come hard with your attempts
to stop me.
You are not dealing with a wimp or no easy hit,
I'm a fighter with God in my corner
as my trainer.
There is not a challenge I will back down from.
I will use my achievement as a gun to shoot
every form of negativity
and hear say that comes.
I'm destructive.
Unlike the Terminator,
I won't be back because that would involve me
leaving in the first place.

Yet I proceeding,
proceeding to be what you will despise
to see.
Ultimately the best that I can be.
I live my life boldly with no regrets,
refusing to allow anything to block me.
So get ready to eat your words
and take a humble bow,
because I coming hard
and I'm about to shut it down.

www.ingramcontent.com/pod-product-compliance
Lightning Source LLC
Chambersburg PA
CBHW050015040726

47599CB00014B/1384